Love's Brutal Good Karma

by Becky Orbe

LOVE'S BRUTAL GOOD KARMA

Cover Artwork: Annicka Soriano
Email: annicka.soriano@yahoo.com

Becky Orbe
Website: www.beckyorbe.com

For my Lola Marina, my grandmother, the first person who would have read this book and the first person who found out I dreamed of publishing my own book. Lola, you always said Lolo loved writing too.

CONTENTS

INTRODUCTION

To whoever finds this:

You're allowed to have a past. You're allowed to have a past that you thought would last forever... but didn't. You're allowed to write about how happy you felt, that it brought you so much hope. You're allowed to have fairytale ideals, to let it all crumble down from all the heartbreaks, and then reconstruct it all again when you know better.

You might get it wrong a bunch of times, but I hope that you always remember this:

YOU CAN NEVER GO WRONG WHEN YOU CHOOSE TO LOVE.

1

LOVE'S ROSE-COLORED BRUTAL LESSONS

The Liberty

It was raining in Midtown that night
And my friends made a run for it.
A crowded place, but I saw your face
And then I thought, "Don't count on it,
you're not his type.
You're not his type."

But I left The Liberty with you.

People can stay in your life for a really long time
Even if you expect them to leave
The moment you meet.

Un-Drunken Night

Beer bottle I knock over on the bench
I promise I wasn't drunk
I just couldn't pull myself together,
Hyperaware of being around you.
Paper towels you had to get from the kitchen
I promise nobody has ever had to clean up after me

I walk through the bathroom door
Concerned faces from friends stare at me
Standing by the bedroom door
You knew something was up
I rush to your side and ask if we could leave

Something about your thumb
Playing, circling around my knuckles
Made me feel better
After embarrassingly throwing up
In Leonard's Tudor City bathroom

Something about your arms
Snaking around me
Your hand on my back soothing me
In the middle of a fast-food chain
Waiting for my coffee and your midnight snack
Made me feel all right

I don't ever get tired of walking
Whenever it's you I'm with,
Even when I've had too much to drink
Because you held me by the hand at the beginning of fall
And held me by the heart at the end of winter.

Instead of looking back
At this un-drunken night
As the time you didn't even
Check up on me if I got home,

It was a memory of how you saw
An unbecoming side of myself
And made the best out of it

Now you tell me to eat first
And drink a lot of water
When I'm drinking beer

It was just too bad we didn't finish
The 12-pack beer
You bought for me.

It Was All Enough

I remember how I always waited for the signs
Still learning to walk to the beat of this city.
But then you took me by the hand
And that's how I learned to dance
Gracefully through these mean streets.

Less than an hour after just meeting you,
I learn that you like wine
And honestly it takes me back to the one before
Because we both loved beer.
But sooner or later I realize this isn't a matching game.

I love Tuesdays
Because I know you are just on the opposite side
of the 5th floor
But I admit that every time I buy my iced coffee across the
street before class,
I hope I don't bump into you
Because my heart always does strange things around you.

No promises
But it was all enough for me
Whenever you walked through that strange corner on the
5th floor,
Hands in your pockets,
A boyish smile,
And brown eyes that sometimes look golden
Meeting mine.

I don't think I even breathe
every time we catch the elevator down,
You, standing so close next to me
As the last crowd ends the day
In this sleepless city.

One Last Walk In Midtown

If I knew then that was going to be our last walk in
Midtown,
The last time we'd share an elevator,
The last time we'd exit 11 West 42 together

The last time I'd walk beside you,
The last time I'd hear you talk non-stop,
The last time I'd look up to your brown eyes while you did

The last time my arms would accidentally brush against
yours,
The last time you'd be walking too close next to me,
The last time you'd want me to walk with you until 33rd
Street,
The last time I'd have to stop myself from wanting too

The last time we'd say "see ya" in that corner of Bryant Park,
The last time I'd wish you'd come after me,

I wouldn't ever do it any different
I wouldn't be sad about it
I wouldn't regret any of it
I wouldn't do more,
Even if I knew it was the last time.

(Continued on the next page)

Because in those little moments we shared,
Those short walks
Those awkward silences in the elevators
Those accidental brushes of our arms
Those non-stop talks you shared,
That Jersey accent that made it hard for me at times to keep
up

That was what made us…
Us.

"You Look So Cool"

I love how you stopped asking me to come home with you.
I love how you walked to the ice cream shop with me
even if you didn't buy any.
I love every time we walk out of our classes
in Midtown together.
I love how you were easily just a friend
I love how you stopped flirting with me aggressively.

Maybe we really weren't right as lovers,
But as friends,
We're pretty cool
Just like my favorite line
In that song, "Robbers" by The 1975.

I love the rush of this blind optimism that I will deny
No, I don't see you as a friend,
I still feel tense around you

I love the thrill of the danger,
The price I'm going to pay in pain,
The recklessness,
The carelessness.

One day I know I will wake up
And grow up
But after being sheltered for so long,

I need to learn my lesson first
I need to make my mistake first
I need to know if you're a mistake
first.

Barge Into My Life

Maybe it wasn't goodbye after all,
But why is the universe playing tricks
On our minds again?
What is the point of all of this
If I'm not going to think about
The possibilities of us?

The main question is why.

Why are we suddenly here?
Why have you made your presence felt again
After months of nothing

After I've cried over you
After I've battled my demons of you
After coming to terms with myself
After healing myself
After that epiphany I had
Why are we still in each other's minds?

Nobody comes back over and over again
Like the way you have repeatedly
Barged into my life.

I'm terrified of the same mistakes
I'm terrified of making wrong decisions
I'm terrified if you're still the same person
I'm terrified of the next move I'll make
I'm terrified of what this all means.

But why do you repeatedly barge into my life?
People come and go
But you still haven't.

But until when again?
What does the clock say
On the time left
Until you are bored of me
Again?

But barge into my life
Because I would like to find out.

Even If You Go

I remember thinking how you would
eventually leave me the night we met,
And it terrifies me that you still haven't yet.

We've been through a lot in between;
A lot of back-and-forth
A lot of second-guessing
A lot of figuring each other out
And a lot of disappearing acts.
In some ways, I just want you to finally do it.

Because it frightens me that you're still here.
When you should have been LONG GONE.

I want to surround myself with positive thoughts
But that would have to include you
and all the possibilities of us.

Leave me here while you're not even mine
to lose
Disappear for good when I don't even get
to choose.

I want you to, so badly.
Because there's a part at the back of my mind
That's small enough to go unnoticed
But strong enough to give hope.
I want you to leave for good
But that small voice is just screaming for you to
Stay from now on.

I'm afraid you'll disappear again
and I would hate myself for believing this time
would be different.

But there will always be that ruling part of me
that chooses to love deeply.
Even if that means hoping excessively,
Even if that means hurting extravagantly.
My choice will always be to love.

So even if you go,
I would have gained another person
In my long list of people
Who I cared about
And you would have lost someone
who genuinely
Loved you.

Not Even You

No matter how many times you abandon me,
I will always welcome you back
As I vowed to myself that I will be different,
Set apart
From all the women you're so used to leaving
Who never let you in again when you try to come back
Because maybe you also never do.

I will be that one person who will always see
The good in you
I will be the one friend you will have
Even when everyone leaves you behind

That's why I was never afraid
Of my wholesome motivational nothings;
The ones you get before 6:20 pm

That's why I was never afraid
You'd think I was too into you
As I checked on you the night after
Sneezing the whole way to get my coffee ice cream

Even when you didn't check on me
After I threw up at Leonard's
Even when you made me feel
That you couldn't care less.

Because I know how it feels
To be not thought of,
To be not cared about.
And I wouldn't want that
To happen to anyone.
Not even you.

Withdrawals

Forget about how I wouldn't belong in your world;
How I might not get along with your friends,
How we might not have the same values,
And how we're simply incompatible.

When it comes to withdrawals,
None of the sensible things matter.
Everything feels perfect and high
Like morphine taking away the pain.

Oh how I wish I could see you
for just another day.

One Day I Will See

Bryant Park's trees were suddenly greener
The summer I had to let go.
Drowning epiphanies in the form of a poem
About how I almost flew back home.

Seven days a week secretly praying
I'll get to see you sooner than never
In one of the masked faces
I'll bump into in school.

I would have no problem identifying
Which one you are despite the coverings.
I have known your warm brown eyes
For about a year now.

They have haunted me
since you disappeared on me
The way this generation does it.

They have haunted me
when you came back—
how I never really learn.

My imagination goes into a frenzy
Every time you reappear out of thin air;
Wild possibilities, making my heart race
Desirous fantasies that could happen in reality.

(Continued on the next page)

I've grown tired of playing games,
Yet here I am always so helpless
Whenever you give me an idea
That you want me.

I lie in my bed breathing heavily
Imagining if I can simply exhale you
out of my system.
But you have affected me too deeply
That you have stained my blood.

One day I will see
That my expectations will never see light.

I could be wrong, I could be right.
The future was never something
anyone had accurately figured out.
So for now,
I think I'll just enjoy the ride.

Hidden Items

Jet lag from a plane abroad
Yankee pen you already lost

2 am who do you call?
Do you remember calling me that night at all?

High-fives and teases
There lay our hidden feelings
Buried them deep
Until we feel less

Blue scarf, donut hat
Distractions on worst days we ever had

Stanford shirt; tucked out white
This is how we've felt for a while
Bottled up in a jar
Finally stopped talking in your car

Bay water brought clarity
Current driving us deeper into the woods
Oh, the romantic irony

Champagne nights, hotel rooms
First and last I spent beside you

Makeup off, you didn't care
As well as the shirts that I wear

(Continued on the next page)

21

Sunlight through windows, you look at me
I lie remembering how I'll say goodbye
Before breakfast and coffee

Handwritten letter
You saw hidden in your gift
Is that why you didn't open
When everyone else did?
Three pages
I've run out of time to say
Hugged me twice in the dark
Left you in a wine bar

Newfound man who loves wine
Brown eyes made me feel fine.
Did you ever feel my pain?
I keep writing poems of him on the train

Privacy contrasting yours
Overshare, back and forth
Over-flooded, truth sets me free
I fancy how you both feel

I do believe she's the one
Pretty sure she has given back
The kisses you stole
When we were sitting in the stack

Hidden in pain, the timing was right
Honored if I was the last you loved
Before you met
The love of your life.

20 Years

Traffic jams, late for school
Two moms running to get their kids inside
That's how you and I walked side-by-side
Holding hands,
I somehow still feel it.

Nosy little girl minds your business
Tells you how to hold a crayon bossily
Would you have learned how to write
If it weren't for me?

Say I'm not your best friend but there's no point
When someone claws their way back into your life
That said enough.
Would we have seen each other again
If I didn't look you up on the Internet?

First date of my life in my favorite mall
After you played basketball
Watched a movie of my favorite superhero
Asked if I was cold, I said "No."
Would you have put your grey jacket around me
If I had said I was?

In our school's chapel, I cry pleading Him
Four signs I left up to fate
"All-or-nothing" was the deal I made.
You showed up at my grandma's house
Having all the right pieces

(Continued on the next page)

A black suit, a black tie, white shirt
There was one thing missing
And I had to keep my tears in
As you held out the white corsage.
Paris was where you brought me
In a very familiar place
I spent years of my brother's family days.

Matthew was the name of your friend
You asked me to dance with him and he flirted.
Would you have not gotten jealous
If you had just asked me to dance with you
When that was the only thing I wanted?
All night I waited for you to.

All the people I love around me,
Room dressed up in New York,
I know it would have been great
If you had given me a rose
But would you have even gone to my 18th
If it did not fall on your brother's birthday?

Blocking was the language I never expected you to teach me
But did you know that I was mad
Only because you were the one person
I wanted there so bad?

Desperate wrong move to get over you
I pursue a boyfriend for barely a month
Who cursed you because he knew
To me it was always going to be you.

Graduation caps and tassels
One last chance to see you
You go another direction instead of where I tell you to go.
I scream and curse you and tear up
Alli hugs me and tells me to finally let go.
We get in the crowded elevator
My phone rings, a message that says, "I'm here."
Like a movie scene, time stood still
Doors started to close, time to decide
What do you do?
Go.

I stopped believing in signs after you
But it's part of growing up,
Not really an issue.

And like karma tying up the ends,
You thank me for everything, on my birthday
Having just read my musings that say
How much I truly loved you all this time.

Questions, rhetorical or not,
I know that not a lot
Are lucky enough like us to be twenty-four
And have a friend you have known
For twenty years long.

New Year's Eve

I took the last cab going to St. Mark's Place
The last one that gets you where before midnight
The last one you'd be lucky enough to hail
The last one the devils and angels save just for you.

Counted down the seconds with you
When no one else did
From twenty to one
A new year has begun.

Wouldn't have it any other way
Wouldn't have wanted you to kiss me
If you weren't going to mean it anyway
If you didn't mean *any of it* anyway.

I was happy there in that moment
That's all that mattered.
Gone was my routine of thinking about
This was the year of what I'd accomplish.

All I was thinking was how
I am spending this midnight with you
My favorite holiday.

Fireworks went off
Reflected on your windows
I ran up the rooftop to catch it;
I didn't.
Neither did you
Bother to catch me.

Winter In Forest Hills

It's 10 am you packed up my bedroom
Remember building forts here
Under grey bedsheets
Pounding from below
And I said you couldn't stay…
But I wanted you to.

You started shoveling the snow
Right outside my new place
"Where'd you find a guy like this?" they said
And I wish that I could say
That you were mine.

I never learned how to play my cards right
I let it all go, I was always in control
And now I think,
How did we get this far?

It's winter in Forest Hills
Snow covers every inch of pavement
I'm blasting out Christmas songs for you
You don't like it but let me show you
What it's like to be loved by me
Your present underneath the tree

I called you out from my bedroom window
Like a kid I teased you
Playing hide and seek
I wish you played along,
Didn't want to let it go…

27

Because we both know you used to.

I poured a warm cup of water for you
Showed how much I cared
You took just one sip
Then shooed me away
My landlord smiled at me and said,
"I'm sure he appreciates it."

It's winter in Forest Hills
Snow melting from the warmth that you brought in
I'm sending out the Christmas spirit for you
You finally told me how much it meant to you
What it's like to be loved by me
"Somewhere in my memory"
A video from you Christmas morning

I know you got burned and now it's me you can't trust
But you haven't met
Someone who loves so unconditionally
Would care for your time to heal
Would care for fragility
I swear it's not too good to be true!

HELP ME PLAY MY CARDS RIGHT!
GIVE US JUST MORE TIME!
GIVE US THIS REAL CHANCE!
HELP ME HELP YOU HEAL FROM THE SCARS
THEY JUST LEFT YOU!

And we'll see that one day
We'll look back on Moving Day
See how in the beginning
We didn't have to be afraid!

Seasons changed and so did my address
Congratulating myself
This is the longest
Anyone has stayed.
LONGEST ANYONE HAS STAYED!

It's winter in Forest Hills
Please stay for longer so you will see
What it's like to be loved by me.

It's winter in Forest Hills
I haven't heard from you for days now…

…

What's it like to be loved by you?

The Night I Ruined It All

Met you at John Street
Ballot in your hand
The nine-hour lunch date that we never planned
Didn't feel a thing
But then you called me every night

Met your friends
In Downtown
Welcomed me with open arms
Only been a week
But I think this could work out

Dressed in disguise
The city's lit tonight
Brooklyn Bridge is dazzling on your window side
Fragile little heaven
But if only I had known
That would be the night
I would ruin it all

The night I ruined it all
You held me by the hand
In that taxicab
On our way back home

(Continued on the next page)

You met my friends at dinner
We're back in Midtown
Where the rooms start burning up
With smoke around
Now you're overthinking
Because of what I said

I held on longer than I should have stayed
Because 57th Street had its way
So if we had a lovely night
Tell me why your walls are up
That's why I look back to that night

The night I ruined it all
You held me by your side
In our movie night
And when I said
"I wanna do this right."

I never told you why I hugged you
In that elevator ride
I wanted to run far as fast as I can
Away from what you made me feel
I was scared.
Later that night everything was alright.

Unfiltered and honest conversations
I didn't know it was a trap for my demise
The only reason why I told you those things
You saw right through me and broke down my walls

(Continued on the next page)

Maybe it was all meant to be
We were already doomed from that night!

Dressed in disguise
The city's lit tonight
Brooklyn Bridge is dazzling on your side
Broken little heaven
Now I see where I went wrong
Maybe I WANTED TO
RUIN IT ALL!

The night I ruined it all…

Run as fast as I can.

My love doesn't pick people.
It just clings on to you
When you treat me right
Even at the bare minimum.

It's the one thing I'm good at…

It's the one thing we all know how to do

Our Time Is Almost Up, Isn't It?

For the first time,
I know how the story is about to go
And yes,
it's easier to rid at this point.

"All women love blue eyes,"
But all I could see were
Flashes of brown eyes that turned golden
Through 6th Avenue's lights,
Dilated.

Brush in front of the mirror and
Make sure your hair falls just right
Covering most of your neck
As it always has.

Strange familiarity with what comes next
Hovers above my head
The violent rush lingers even as I wake
Was it a dream or was it real?

And if I didn't know better
I think I just
Ruined it all again.
I think I knew
That I would once again.

(Continued on the next page)

"It's okay to admit what you want"
But I have to learn from a while ago
Honesty was the trap for my demise.
That's why I don't say it out loud.

And for some reason in my instinct
I think this time it is different
But I have to know better
Than to trust my optimism.
I guess it's getting closer now
To skepticism.
I should know better
That the time from then to now
Is the time minds make up
And the end of the day
Should be no surprise.

It's an endless paradox
Of my guilt and my inhibitions;
How my own nature
Is constantly at war
And I understand now
I won't get so far
At least in the near future.

I'll write another poem one day
That will prove myself right
Because I should know
Better by now.

INT. THE RUSSIAN TEA ROOM — NIGHT

Friday the 13th. In a pandemic. A calamitous fate of another shutdown is close to inevitable.

Upon entering, a piece plays over the restaurant's quiet sound system. Barely three notes, she recognizes the composition immediately like it's more than human nature—it pulsates like her blood vessels; the ones that keep her love for cinema alive.

Comptine d'un autre été l'après-midi. The beautiful piece from the film, Amelie.

She feels a sudden rush of emotions—it's irony, poetic cinema, imminent bliss, and insurmountable imperturbability—all at once.

Ghosts of past memories and stories linger in the restaurant. She just doesn't know it yet. She just doesn't know it yet that a voice will speak to her in the bathroom and beg the question:

Does she really want to leave a memory of her saying goodbye to him? Or will she leave the memory of how this was the night she decided to stay? Take the shortcut and be one step closer to finding the right one? Or take love fully; happiness, bruises, cuts and all until the very end?

2

THE DECONSTRUCTION AND
RECONSTRUCTION OF IDEALS

Time Was Up For A While Now

I do know better now.

How we sat then
And how I stood now,
Towering over you
A telling image
I had power now.

"I was thinking about it…"—Just stop.
You don't even need to make an effort
To keep going
And keep defending
And keep explaining
It's echoing
I've heard this spiel before
I'm tired
It's the same predictable screenplay

But at the back of my mind
I'm grinning with pride
Just because as you speak
I now know
And I saw it coming
Not like how it broke me before.

(Continued on the next page)

I use it now as an ace
Because you didn't know
How it would turn out,
Yet I was already here
Two weeks ago
And it feels so good

In my mind, it had already ended then.
There's always a ticking time bomb,
A countdown timer over your heads
And I'm always waiting for it to go off
Because when did it not?
It's all I've ever known.

For an optimist
This is where I'm most skeptical
But I think it's important for me to be
Because I love
Like I have never loved
Before.

Downtown

It's Tuesday
I'm on my way home from Downtown
I took the E Train at World Trade Center
I sit too comfortably;
It's a long way home.

But I like coming from Downtown.

Tonight I take away from my reverie
Anything that even just the slightest
Touched the thought of him
Touched the thought of the next one.

I'm tired.
Maybe this time I've really had enough
Or it's just another one of those times
And one day I'll have another relapse
Taking me back to square one.

But tonight there's a strange peace
In the air, in myself,
Or maybe just in this nearly empty car.

I can feel my hands flexing
Even just a bit, letting go of something
And I try to refocus on what mattered

This city is what I fell in love with
It was the most powerful thing
That the universe conspired.

Our Conversation on March 29, 2021

I'm sitting in shock
After I hang up
From a conversation that was
actually good.

Yet I am trying to pick up pieces of myself.

Diary Poem: September 12, 2021

"Cut them off, it's easier."
Sure, it is.
But I hope one day
You are with the right people
And you'll get to see for yourself
How wonderful life is
When you don't allow yourself
To focus on faults,
Hate, anger, and bitterness.
It takes time,
but you'll get there just fine.
And it's all because
They make it easy for you
To hold on to them.
Because they hold on to you
too.

Darling Girl,

Darling girl,

Love in your own terms.
In your own timing
In your own pace
In your own liking.

Love like how your 12-year-old self dreamed of being loved.

Show it off
Or protect it at all costs
Just remember:

You don't owe anyone
anything.

Thank You For Not Showing Up

Thank you for not showing up
When you were the one person
I wanted there
On my 18th birthday.
Even if you had your reasons
And it broke my heart,
I understand now
Why I should thank you.

Thank you for not showing up
On my 25th birthday
Because you couldn't drop everything
For a couple of minutes on the train
And a couple of minutes at my party,
Letting me know I am not a priority.

Thank you for suddenly disappearing
Only to resurface again
And disrupt my headway.
The push and pull I'll never know
How I crawled out of the dead weight.

Thank you for forgetting
And making it feel like
I really never was worth your time
And even headspace;

For destroying that last 0.0001%
of hope
That made everything still stand strong;
The remaining holding brick
In the castle of fantasy
I built for my own grave.

Do you really think
I wouldn't find love
in this damned city?
The ones who believe that
are the ones who make it so.
The ones who don't
make it beautiful with their souls.

She Belongs To Me

She was pure
She was a jewel
She was a natural.
She dreamed
She believed in impossible things
She knew exactly what she wanted to be.

She ran as fast as she can
She was focused
She was hard on herself
She was a perfectionist
She knew exactly what to look for.

Yet you punished her exactly for that.
For not finding love at 21
You said her standards are too high
And she should lower it down.

So as time passed
And she kept being entwined
With the wrong people,
She became the one who tolerated red flags
Telling herself it's called empathy.

She hurt herself more
For defending the wrong people
As she wore rose-colored glasses.
It didn't hurt like one big painful heartbreak
After breaking up with a long-term partner
(Continued on the next page)

For her, it happened little by little
What they call
Death by a thousand cuts,
Because as each scar barely heals,
She reattaches herself again
Thinking it was never there.

She started believing
She ruins everything
And she never gets it right
When the only common denominator
Has always just been compatibility
Of both sides.

You will never know
How painful it was to get her back
Just for slightly believing you
And being open to your ideas,
Even if you read this.

Know that your words were poison
That slowly spread through her bloodstream
Each and every time
It was just not the right person.

I wish she was the last one you punished
For knowing exactly what she wanted.
I say sorry to her that I didn't protect her
Enough.
I wish you never said those things
Never implanted those toxic ideas into her

Because she wasn't yours to condescend
She wasn't yours to protect,
She saves herself.

She knew exactly what she wanted
And from that you should have known
She will be more than FINE
Wherever she goes.

She wasn't yours to poison
With your reality that wasn't hers.
She wasn't yours to lose,
She was MINE.

SHE BELONGS TO ME.

Childhood Stories

When I was a child
My fingers accidentally got caught in the elevator doors.
I screamed and cried,
My dad trying to budge it free.

I hopped on the hotel elevator,
The one we weren't supposed to take
And when the doors were closing,
I forced it open with my tiny arms
For irrational fears that I would never find my family again.
Elevators traumatized me.

When I was twenty-one years old
I tried to force open a glass door to my dreams
And the gatekeeper let me know
I won't have to stand outside forever,
There's a way in.

At twenty-three years old
I run to catch trains
And every time the doors nearly close on me
I force them open with my still tiny arms
With all the strength my body could summon,
Jumping in, out of breath,
all eyes on me that say,
"She made it."

She was the same girl
traumatized by elevator doors.

And all this time
I grew up learning how to fight hard,
With a spirit bigger than five-foot-one.
Closed doors tried to keep me scarred
But it just made me want things more.

To keep wanting to barge into every room
To keep believing I belonged in every single one of them
To keep refusing to accept that doors won't open.

Little Miss Perfect

Little Miss Perfect did everything right.
Little Miss Perfect shined bright like the sun.
Little Miss Perfect never went out at night.

Little Miss here are my boundaries.
Little Miss the night wasn't for her
Until her confidence paid the price

And then she realized she shined like a star
In even the darkest night.

Little Miss Did Everything Right.

Little Miss biggest fear is making mistakes because of it
Little Miss depressed because perfection was the only
standard she's ever known
Little Miss calculated and afraid to try new things.

Little Miss made those mistakes
Little Miss deconstructed ideals that needed to break.

Make Your Own Rules

Everybody will tell you how it should be,
Another emphasis on how
You're not cut out
For this world

But darling,
When you know you have something
So true,
Real, and beautiful,

By all means,
Make your own rules
Defy odds and expectations
Be the exception
That inspires the world
To believe
That good things happen.

The Unknown

I've spent the past few weeks
Thinking I was in the dark
Trying to navigate life
A bit blindly
Being led by only pieces of answers
Until I find the light
At the end of the tunnel

Then I realized that
The way I have been approaching this darkness;
Not taking for granted
The great things that are at present
happening to me in the background,
That somehow,
Someway,
Overpowers the grave monster
Lurking in the dark.

I haven't been completely in the dark.
Like flames from matches,
I have amazing people around me
Who try to help me find the answers
To shine a light just far enough
To get me to the next step.

It's dark in here;
I don't have the answers,
I don't see the big picture yet.
But these matches don't seem to die quickly
In an instant

And disappear.

The Snake Sheds at Breakfast

I wasted breakfast in a place I called home
With the cynic and his closed-off mind
That tried to force ideals about personal affairs
While he goes back to his old habits
Of laying in bed with someone
As long as he self-sabotages
In two months.

Sorry—was that too real?
I didn't mean to have a forked tongue
To deceive anyone of
The kind reputation that precedes me
But I think it's time that side of me
Slithers in
When all I have wanted was peace
But the hunters lurk with their noses
Up my own nesting sanctuary.

Somehow I became fluent now
From the tactic I did two years ago
Either easier through time
Or easier because of the natural instincts
More overprotective than I ever was.

She Will Find It One Day

She will find it one day.
No matter how many times she's been hurt,
no matter how many times she gives all her love
No matter how many times
she daydreams about the endless possibilities
No matter how many times
the reality fails her optimistic expectations
She will find you one day.

She will be tall enough to do it right
because of all the hurt she has gone through;
because of all the hurt she is still about to go through.

But one day, the sun will shine its brightest,
Just like the kind of sunshine she just wanted to bring
into the lives of every man she's ever loved

But it will be a different kind of daylight;
It will be the one that illuminates her life
It will be the one that makes everything make sense.

Too Picky

I was told I was too picky
That I could never hold a relationship
Past two
Or even a month.

I wasn't picky.
In fact, a very few found it as someone
Who knew exactly
What she wanted.

So when I found the right one,
I knew.
Immediately.

Only For Those Who Get Older

I chase you down like a cat
And after the third try
I knew I would get tired
But I never wished for you
To chase me down
And I would be the one who wouldn't care.
I never wished for it
Because I knew I would already be at peace with it.

The things you have left to talk about
Show you don't know me at all
Even after all this time
And the song goes, you will never know.
I can count the things you associate me with
With just a single hand,
You agreed communication is key
But you never had it with me.

Your desperation shows and I don't want *any* of it.

What were you expecting from someone
You treated like an option?
That you could pull her back within arms reach
And only pay attention at your convenience?

(Continued on the next page)

Maybe you didn't know
Or maybe you only paid attention to yourself.
She brought her standards down
When she moved to this town
Just because everybody told her
She was too high to reach.

But before you, she commanded crowds
With her own personality that never frowned,
She broke records and she climbed the highest grounds.
What did you expect from the youngest girl
Who moved eight thousand miles away from everyone she
knew?
That was her at 23,
Imagine what she's unafraid to do at 26.
Did you think that was easy
Just as you thought she was easy?

She is making it out here alone
In a land she has the audacity
To call her home
Because she has owned her place
Storming into every room in this city.

She is so much higher than you
That she stooped down to your level
Just for you to like her.
It's the truth and it's not one you want to hear
But then again, it only stings
when the shoe fits.

At the end of the day,
You will focus on how she was so into you,
That she chased you,
And she put you on a pedestal;
Oh, how you are God's gift to women.
Ironically those who rightfully hold it true
Would never think like you.

In retrospect, I wouldn't stop her.
Because she laid her cards down
In front of you,
The brave thing that she did
To get the job done.
You couldn't have done that
Because the mixed signals of the game
Is where you keep your ace.

All games come to an end
Only for those who get older
So that begs the question:

When you wonder why,
Remember that when she laid her cards down,
That was when you told her
This was exactly what you wanted.

Maybe it stings that it came from her,
Not you.

(Continued on the next page)

You, who thinks this is a checkmate
When it really doesn't matter.
She was never one to play games
But in just treating you well
So in the end,
it was she who prevailed.

She doesn't want any of this attention
You're constantly invading her with now,
It's all tainted from knowing
This is how you speak every time
Boredom strikes.

Who would have thought?
She wouldn't have.
It just came naturally.
She's ruled by the planet Saturn.
You know what Saturn is also known as?

The Lord of
Karma.

All games come to an end
Only for those who get older.

For The Love Of My Life

Isn't it supposed to be as easy as
Not having to do anything;
That even if you try to avoid me,
Destiny will always rearrange the universe
for you to find your way back to me?

I've walked through this life
Believing in signs and destiny and
fairytale endings,
Walked long enough finding nothing,
to let go of that and stop believing,

Obsessively trying to find it in a man
Who doesn't nearly give a damn.
Making excuses and creating chances
always thinking, "just in case".

I try to draw fine lines
to keep myself intact and sane.

My impatience is seen
in countless pages of poems
intensively written
for the wrong man.

There's nothing more that I want
Than to write all these beautiful words
that paint vivid imagery of love
For you.

(Continued on the next page)

How do you write about something
You've never felt?
So I keep writing poems about him instead.

This one,
I tried writing about you.

3

HOW SHE ALMOST LEFT TRILOGY

How She Almost Left

When she thought she had let go,
her demons came sitting down at the table,
Eager to feast with her, pretending they never left.
Overpowered the impulse to bury them,
she welcomed them back instead.
They pleaded that they had something to say:

"It's only when you dance with us
that you will get to see the truth,
that your hands had now grown numb
from tightly grasping on to the control,
disguising as a feeling of letting go."

The winds blew an air of darkness
and with it, a plane to fetch her.
She's up in the air without a single luggage in hand
But in her heart she keeps countless memories
Of inside jokes, brown eyes,
and Midtown streetlights in two different seasons.

One final act to push him away for good
Or one final shot at hope for him to stay
from now on.

In effortless choices of loving and of seeing the good in
people,
She knew she would suffer the same fate
twice, even thrice.

In memory of tediously drawn blueprints,
Names of kingdom rulers,
And running as fast as she can,
What once defined her were stripped off her,
Leaving her to die in the naked truth.

In the darkest hour,
the creatures echoed a resonating eulogy:
"You have danced so gracefully on your own
through every brutal and deafening sound
this city could unforgivingly hurt you with.
And you will do it again with a stronger fight."

At the break of dawn,
she sharply gasps the breath of her rebirth.
Tears run down her face
And with it was an inner peace of knowing

That the love she keeps giving out unconditionally
Will one day karmically and sacredly return to her
barging in without any warning,
just as how she has stormed
into every room in this city:
bravely and unapologetically.

In the darkest times,
That's when she knew
For better, for worse,
Where and why she truly belonged.

In fight or flights, she lost.
In sink or swims, she sank.
And in her drowning death,
When she finally stopped fighting the waves,
When she finally stopped struggling for breath,
That's how she survived.

How They Stayed

When she did let go,
her demons drew up her gray curtains,
letting the daylight in, during her darkest night.
Overpowered by all she's ever known
that people come and go,
Her demons enwreathed her with people she could hold.

"You have learned to let go of control
And now the truth terrifies you to the soul.
But it's time you learn now than someday,
Run as fast as you can,
but never away."

Seasons changed the air of darkness
and with it, clear skies and the plane she never boarded.
She was underwater because she learned to survive
But the waves brought her to shore,
Continuing stories of inside jokes, brown eyes,
And new 57th Street narratives with cancelled goodbyes.

One final act to push him away was no good
One final shot at hope she let go
Still he chose the same,
from now on to stay.

In effortless choices of loving and of seeing the good in
people,
Not again would she have to suffer
twice, even thrice—
They proved her wrong.

Rejoice to the mistakes she finally let herself make,
Quiet nights she finally let herself indulge in,
And forgiving herself to walk so she can run again.
What she tried so hard to perfect
Was carefully stripped off by the people around her,
Reminding her that her flesh was human.

At the height of sunlight,
the creatures sang an ode to her scars,

"You have danced so bravely into the unknown,
Opened your eyes to the realness brought in by the storm,
Saw the world was not simply black and white.

And it was in that gray area;
where empathy was always seen as making excuses,
where seeing the good in people was always seen as naiveté,
that was where you found
Where the good things hide."

In the morning light,
she rises from the shore, sand beneath her feet.
Tears run down her face
And with it was a smile, finding

As karmically and as sacredly as she had hoped,
The love she wanted to find in just one she did not,
But what she found in them
Felt like it barged into her life
At the right time when she protected her world
And went to the right place where the good things hide:
in simply choosing to love.

In dark clouds and rain in Montauk,
In unprojected clear skies on the esplanade,
In a table for eight in a Midtown French restaurant,
In a backyard in Forest Hills,
She would never know
If she never wrote that poem.

In un-boarded flights, her death.
In writing words of pain, her rebirth.
And when she finally stopped dreaming
Of how she could be loved one day
only by the one,
When she opened the doors for them,
When they chose with her to stay,

That's how she was loved.

Karmically and Sacredly

Isn't it amazing how one person was not meant to show up
So you could finally realize how tired you were
How ready you were to try again
Just to be let down again
And confirm everything you have learned
From patterns of their own kind
Thinking you were in a powerful position
Because you were wiser
Because you saw it coming
Only to realize you've become pessimistic
About the one thing you believed in
Because you were waiting for it to happen;
You were looking for the worst things now
When you have always looked for the good things
Even when they always did you wrong.
So you shutdown -r
Because you did not like the person you were becoming.
And when you gave up trying
And flew back to the waters to drown again,
When you were the most pessimistic about love
But didn't want to be,
That was when all you've ever wanted
Karmically and sacredly
Barged into your life without any warning,
Just as how you have stormed
Into every room in this city:
Bravely and unapologetically.

4

THE LOVE THAT KARMICALLY AND SACREDLY COMES BACK

Little Italy

I took my mom here
(the last time I was with anybody
here).

"That's where they shot the baptism scene,"
I point her
The reason why I go here
And not anywhere else.

I go on intentional trips to Little Italy
Hoping every single time
It was empty
So I could speak my thoughts
Out loud
Crying

Today
I'm here again
With somebody
This time

God knows
What I've been asking for
Over and over again
And what I cannot ask for
Are the same thing.

We sat at the front
We both look up
Almost to the vault

I believe
I brought the right person
With me
But in the end
I don't
Have a say,
I speak out
Silently.

And in that moment
All of my fears
Anxieties
Worries
I've been bringing
With me
Here
For the past 2 years
Were nowhere
To be found.

I'm Finally Tired

I think I'm finally tired
Of trying to do it right
Maybe we never do in a lifetime
But we can always try

I met you on a Sunday afternoon
Hopped on a railroad
Where the Hempstead led me to the wrong
Maybe the Babylon was the right one all along

Took me to the beach and walked on the boardwalk
Found the edge of the sand
That was when we took our shoes off

If I wanted to escape
The noise of all my mistakes
I never thought I would have someone
Who would take me exactly where
I needed to be

Where I could hear the waves crashing
Where the sand got my feet sinking
Where I was with just one person
But he was all I needed
For me to breathe

I've seen the beauty
Of brown eyes turning golden
I found a home
in St. Mark's Place, too.

I've become a pessimist
In the chaos of the illusion of control
That I might finally learn it all—
How to do it right this time.

I've become a pessimist
In the midst of trying to get it right
But in the quiet of the daylight
Was where I fell in love with you

I've drowned in the sea and let go
I found myself back on the shore.

Coffee On Saturday Morning

You were in your scrubs
And your glasses on
"Now you've seen me in the morning."

And your comfort and ease
of being able to show me
Made me feel like you were home
more and more.

Your warm smile and kind eyes
as brown as mine
Makes Fall feel like I'm cozied up,
An imaginary snuggle in your arms.

I have been praying for someone like you
For the longest time
And I wake up in the middle of the night
Crying when the fear sets in
That what if I don't do it right?

If it's too good to be true,
Maybe it isn't anymore
Because I've been waiting so long
Enduring such a tiring road
Of pain and struggle and mistakes.

(Continued on the next page)

You've been learning my language
As if it were the easiest lesson
In the world,
Took off our shoes on the boardwalk
So we could walk on sand.
I don't need fancy dinners
I just want peace and you and the waves.

That night I saw in your eyes
You wanted to get closer to me,
And like a coward I scurried away too quick
For fear I make the same mistakes.

Never again, I want to learn.
Never again, I want to be better.
Never again, I want this to last
forever.

Darling, Here's What I've Learned

Darling,
When he is unsure about you
Walk away
When you find the motivation
That you can change his mind.

Darling,
Here's what I've learned:
It shouldn't be so hard;
You don't need to change anyone's mind
When it comes to love.

What's Wrong With You?

You're not allergic to
Gestures of thoughtfulness;
None of the avoidance of gratitude
And the tolerant face that comes with it
Ever happened with you.
What's wrong with you?

We've only gone on
Eight dates
And you didn't run away
with the push and pull
And the beating of the bush

And in the dark of the room
You left your things to let me know
You'd be back here.
What's wrong with you?

"I miss you," I text.
My roommate tells me I shouldn't have.
"I miss you too," you reply.
What's wrong with you?

Karma Never Forgets

Karma can be such a bitch
When you do things for
Hate, revenge, or just stupid games.

Karma can also be a bitch
When all you do is
Try and try and keep trying
To throw good things out there
And then you don't feel her
Returning the favor.

How can you?
When you overlook all the wonderful things
That are happening to you at present
Because the negatives always outweigh
Your gracious emotions.
Don't worry,
it's only human nature.

But one day,
A year from now—
especially a year from now
or maybe even more—
Without any effort from you
Without moving an inch,

Oh, how funny karma sneaks up
And ties lose ends
You never thought
Would be significant enough
To come back to
'

It became so insignificant
Because of your gracious power
To let go of things that hurt you,
That when she dropped the ball,
That was the only time you remembered.

But my oh my,
Never forget
That karma
Never forgets.

Darling, Here's What I've Learned, Vol. 2

Someone once had the gall
To tell me what my timing
Should look like.

And even when at times
I dislike how I don't speak out
And defend myself,
I've grown to know how
Silence is a virtue—
A Lasallian one, at that.

Darling, here's what I've learned:
The ones who always have so much to say
On businesses that aren't theirs
Are the ones who device
Their own demise.

The ones who choose to be silent,
less talk
Are the ones who come out
With karma on their side.

You Were Nowhere In New York

I saw golden eyes in Midtown
I found a home in St. Mark's
Went to the Garden
With the wrong one
Now I know it all happened
'Cause you were nowhere in New York

I've spent much time here
Wondering what was taking you so long.
It all makes sense now;
you were nowhere near
and before this,
you were there in Cali.

But now you are here
in New York.

Darling, Here's What I've Learned, Vol. 3

The thing is, darling,
One day you will find someone
Who will at one point
Save you
And there is perfectly nothing wrong
with that.

But just go and find strength
In knowing you can save yourself.
There is nothing like it
when you find out
what your resilience can do.

There is nothing like
the voice of your conviction.

Warm Hugs

You wrap me with warm hugs
Every time I surprise you
Not like how I've always been
pushed away before.

I finally found someone
Who didn't push me away
Who didn't run away
Who was not afraid
to look me in the eye
To show his heart was full
Whenever I would write
Cheesy cards
Give sweet nothing gifts
Give small surprises

I love being wrapped in your arms
standing for hours
Waiting for the Rockefeller Christmas tree
To light up

No more games,
No more beating around the bush,
Just honesty in what we feel
And taking our time

This is the warmth you feel
when you know that it's real.

The Lottery

Spoke to Him and didn't stop bawling,
I was so in the dark
Even in the mornings.

I never doubted how He listens
And answers
Even if it meant waiting.
But as if He pushed you from your seat,
He called you to rush to me
That same night.

Time stopped as the conversation
went into the depths
Where it would be,
Where you would leave me.

And like an angel
You were right there
Very much decided
About me.

You weren't giving up
And you didn't want to give up.
You still wanted me
Even when everybody says
This would be where it would end.

God sent an angel
Who wouldn't give up on me
When the going got tough,
Who wouldn't leave my side
When my world fell apart,
And who would choose me,
No more questions asked.

It was never about luck
Or chance.
It was always about
What was meant to be.
I won the lottery
The day God sent you
To me.

I Understand Now

Someone asked me today
To explain what I think love is.
I didn't even know where to start
Even with my storytelling smarts.

I understand now
Why you keep some things
A secret for as long as you can,
Why they fumble for words
Just trying to make sense.

How do you get people
Living in a cynical world
To believe that fairytales are real?
To believe chick flick clichés
Aren't just for the movies?
To believe that love really is easy?

I understand now
That when they say you're wrong
You do not owe anyone
Anything
Especially when you have finally found
What you have been looking for
All this time.

Not everyone will be open to believe it
And that's okay.

I understand now
That one of the ways to know
You got it right
Is to get it wrong
A bunch of times.

Never Be Found

All of my days feel like
Two days in one;
One where I wake at 4 am
And one where I wake at 7 am.

I stare at car ceilings
I sleep and I feel like that happened
Yesterday.
The world is asleep
And I'm talking to the streetlights
And shadows
Reflecting on the beige headliner.

Six minutes in a black shell
I'll keep in hushed poems
In dark modes
As we move without the world knowing.

I'll keep stirring riddles
With subliminal messages
That keep the world looking and wondering
While I slyly leave the most important detail
In plain sight.
Everybody saw it months ago
But just didn't know where to look.

(Continued on the next page)

The spotlight shines on
The fifteen-second documentaries with friends
And like a moth to a flame
The world situates and assumes something more
Making it a reality show.
Doesn't matter;
For a while now the real ones have known.
That is where we prevail
In protecting our own world.

Because we are not the light.

We are the sleepy peeking eyes
Checking on the other side of the bed
In the darkness of the room
While the world is still awake
At 9 pm
On a Saturday night.

We are the quiet cozy spot
On the couch
In front of the baseball game on TV,
The dim light that fills the room,
And the hushed voices of The Simpsons
Before I turn it off and close my eyes.

We are the forlorn April night
When I was ready to lose it all
For the hope of it all
And the finger strokes
That broke the fall

We are the nights of frustration
Stuck in the same station
And how I'm allowed to drag it
Because my optimism is understood;
That I get tired
And I'm not okay.

We are the masterpiece behind my phone
Of the boy in the cusp of manhood
Holding an apple
That nobody recognizes
But nonetheless a priceless possession.

We are the sticky messages on the bottle
That never repeat itself,
Stuck on the refrigerator after work.
We are the shadows that walk along the sidewalk
And on morning dews
At 4 am.

We are the stop on the drive back
That doesn't have to be
And the dream that came true
On the sidewalk
Right in front of my house
On a dimly lit street.

We are
What they somehow always believe
Can never be found.

And yet here I am
A hopeless romantic
Who almost believed them,
Writing about it
In the dark.

I Think About You All The Time

When I asked
If you think about me
in the middle of the night,
When the world is asleep
and you're wide awake,
In resting dim lights
or moving through corridors,
In mid-shift meals at 2 am
Or laundry and errands at 3,
You said to me,

"I think about you
All the time."

The Novel

If I were to do exactly
What I set out for myself to accomplish
At 12 years old,
To write full novels
About feelings I felt,

It would all be about you.

And how I knew
Every heartbreak would lead to you.

How I take you to the same meeting place
Where my characters would meet
Down at 78th Street

I would write about how
The chapter I closed
When I hopped on that one-way flight
Was another chapter closer
To the part where I meet you

The rising action would be
How New York was not going down
Without a fight,
On emotional traumas
From players
and the games I let myself
Be foolishly optimistic enough to play.
And how I'll learn just how much—

and I mean SO MUCH—
My emotional endurance can take

And in the falling action
Of defeat,
Or what I now know as peace,
In the M83 song's epilogue:
*Et j'aime comme je n'ai jamais aimé
avant.*
Knowing how to start over
And love like I have never loved
before

Like I have never been scathed
by love before
Like I have never cried over
unrequited love before
Like I have never been frustrated
that it never worked out before
Like I have never blamed my optimism
For being so hopeful about love
Before

The pages will overflow with words
Of my truth in heartbreak
And my truth in staying hopeful

This is the greatest love story
I knew I could write about
One day
As I daydream in my room
At 12 years old.

Well what do you know…
Dreams do come true.

A Fairytale Life

What has life taught me so far?

It's that it can make
All of your dreams come true,
Even the *wildest* ones
That look like fairytales
In your imagination…

But also how not everything
Would come into fruition
According to your ideal vision,
Whimsical imagination,
And daydreamed conceptualizations.

And that's okay.

Because at the end of the day,
I can tell you that
Life still comes through.

And I think that's all that matters.

10 Moons Later

10 moons later,
I find out
my inner voice was right.
I was the luckier one,
after all
Even after losing
The Game of Luck.
The irony of it all
Oh, so beautiful.

Silence my insecurities
And all the elephants in the room
With just a few words.

And I don't believe myself when I say
This one has made up his mind
When everyone else changed theirs in a moment
before

The Cycle Ends With Me

Once upon a time,
A few Thanksgivings ago,
Everything was fine.
I was seeing a guy I liked
'There's no change in his tone,
He's not growing cold,'
I keep my optimism intact.
I tell my friends at dinner
I'm getting happily attached
To something I wasn't open to in the past.

That weekend
When most of the get-togethers were done,
We go on a call:
"I felt something, I'm falling for my friend."
With a smile, my tears don't fall
This isn't the beginning of the end
I had a feeling I've been stalling for a month,
For long

I want to know where I found the strength
To keep smiling and joking
After finding out that someone
Can easily change his mind about me
Just. Like. THAT.
Even when a few days ago we were *fine.*

(Continued on the next page)

I only fall apart
The next time around
And my mind paid for it,
As it tried to survive the suffocating fires
Of scenarios I expected to happen again
Every night.

This isn't the same narrative.
'It's not fair for anyone
Who actually treats you right,'
This is how I trained my mind to fight.

I could retrace and obsess over where it all started
Because I know too well it was in The Liberty,
But there's nothing I can do to take it all back.
That trauma is part of me now
And I was never one to believe in regret.

We can only hope we become the bigger person
With the bigger heart
Who has the strength to not hurt back
Who has the courage to shut down and restart
Every time somebody pulls us apart.

And one day,
When you've turned the grass greener,
You don't have to be lucky to know
That the story always comes to a close
Or even opens to a new prose
With how the "goes around"
Comes around.

I'll Do It Better

How does it feel
To get confused
In the midst of my indifference
And how I no longer care
Like I once did?

You say you're surprised—
that is beyond me—
When in fact
You did the same thing to me
Over and over again.

But I'll do you one better.

I'm not doing it out of boredom
Or the death of the thrill
Or the lack of the chase
And then come back
And do it all over again
As long as you're
within arm's reach.

I'm doing it out of respect
And love.
Not even to get back;
My energy has no time for that.

Because when I walk away,
especially from a bad thing,
I do it for good.

Everything you did,
I'll do BETTER
Because unlike for you,
This is not a game for me.

When You Know

I stopped counting
How many weeks and months
I've been able to do it right
Ever since I knew
it was going to last

You see,
When you've made so many
Different mistakes before,
You'd be surprised how easy it is
To know.

The Little Things

Oh, to have someone
To wake up at 4 am for
To keep company on the road
Just to go back to sleep
10 minutes later.

Oh, to have someone
Who joins you as you hum
"It's Been A Long, Long Time"
As you clean up
After dinner.

Oh, to have someone
To write cheerful sticky notes for
At 5:30 am
When your brain is barely awake

To have someone bake and eat
Brownies with
While watching TV on a Monday.

I Hope They Go Easy On Me When It Happens

Every time I think about
If it would be better
If I stopped keeping this secret
from the rest of the world,

I think about the peace
This life gave for free
Just by keeping it
between you and me,
and our close friends
and families.

I'm not ready for them
To find out just yet.

I'm not ready
For the vultures to come out
and have their fun
Like when they did
When I was 21,
Where my love life
Was everybody's business.

But
I also want to live a life
Where I get to write
About what I love

I want to live a life
Where I get to share
How happy I am
Without having to worry about
The questions people ask

I want to freely share
The magic you and I are making
In this beautiful life
Without having to feel like
I'm giving up
the solitude we built.

I don't know how
Or when I will,
But I think there already is
A sense of being free
As long as it's
You and me.

I just hope
They go easy on me
When it happens
Finally.

The Liberty In Full Circle

Isn't it funny how
In the end,
It was me who pushed you away?

You, who never wanted me
You, who took my kindness for granted
You, who felt like I put you on a pedestal.

Because it's ironic how
The more I treated you well,
The more it hurts you now
When I'm no longer where you kept me:
At arm's length.

I'm somewhere worse for you
But better for me:
Unreachable.

In three years,
I've grown up and the more I knew.
In three years,
You are right where I met you.

My kindness
Might have been taken for granted
By you
But one day, as the air changes,
In the irony of it all,
It is you who will miss me.

Because this world isn't exactly kind
these days.

You will meet more people
Who will think you're not worth the time.
You will meet
Fair-weathered friends
Who don't really give a
Rat's ass about you
Because they aren't "too kind" like me.
And you'll get that sinking feeling
of how you know
I would have been
Evergreen and true.

And you don't have to imagine,
You don't have to guess
How that feels
Because you're already here.

It turns out, my optimism for you
Never turned to an arc.
We only went full circle.
This is right where I met you.

But this time,
instead of leaving with you,

This is where I leave you.

ACKNOWLEDGMENT

This dream truly took a village to actualize. I would not be here without them:

My family, for allowing me to be far from home and live my craziest dreams. My older brother, Raffy, who, in his own brotherly way, showed he supported my writing by teasingly memorizing the names of my fictional characters that I wrote at thirteen years old.

The Lee family, who helped me take the biggest leap of faith to move to New York. I have been waking up every day living my dream because of them.

The love of my life, Chris, for being the living proof that the love that I kept giving out unconditionally, karmically and sacredly did return to me, and exponentially more.

Annicka Soriano, one of my high school best friends, who illustrated the cover of this book and made it even more special. Thank you for giving it the life it deserves.

Felice Neals, who encouraged me and gave me the idea to self-publish. Thank you for leading me to the first step.

My friends, both near and far, for the truest love, support, and understanding that knows no distance.

My past loves, who were lessons I needed to learn, and who became inspirations for these poems.

Mr. Robot and M83, whose art in storytelling and music moved my perspective on life and love.

And my twelve-year-old self, who was crazy and brave enough to dream without limits and had the conviction to believe she could do it. We're doing it, kiddo.

ABOUT THE AUTHOR

Becky Orbe is a Filipino writer and poet based in New York City. She started writing her first novel at twelve years old. Since then, she has dreamed of moving to New York to become a published author. On her way to this dream, she became the Managing Editor at Blue Heights, the official publication of her high school.

She moved from the Philippines to New York at twenty-three years old to take up her Master of Science degree in Integrated Marketing at New York University, still driven by her purpose of fulfilling her dream of becoming a published author. As of writing, she works in the media industry in New York.

"Love's Brutal Good Karma" is her first published book and finally fulfills part of her childhood dream, more than fifteen years in the making. She looks forward to writing more and sharing them with the world.

To learn more about her work, visit www.beckyorbe.com

SCAN AND EXPLORE MORE